wraps

wraps

Jennie Shapter

photography by William Lingwood

RYLAND
PETERS
& SMALL

LONDON NEW YORK

First published in the
United Kingdom in 2007
by Ryland Peters & Small
20–21 Jockey's Fields
London WC1R 4BW
www.rylandpeters.com

10 9 8 7 6 5 4 3 2

Printed in China

ISBN: 978-1-84597-382-7

A CIP record for this book is available
from the British Library.

Senior Designer Toni Kay
Commissioning Editor Julia Charles
Senior Editors
Clare Double, Lesley Malkin
Production Gemma Moules
Art Director Anne-Marie Bulat
Publishing Director Alison Starling

Food Stylist Jennie Shapter
Prop Stylist Liz Belton

Notes
• All spoon measurements are level
unless otherwise specified.
• All eggs are medium unless otherwise
specified. Uncooked or partly cooked
eggs should not be served to the
very young, the very old, those with
compromised immune systems or
to pregnant women.

contents

introduction

Wraps and rolls with tantalizing fillings hidden within are ideal for almost any occasion. Perfect for summertime eating, this collection of recipes includes classic flavours with a modern twist and innovative contemporary combinations inspired by flavours from Europe and the Middle and Far East. Whether you are looking for an appetizer or snack, a selection of light bites for a relaxed gathering or an easy-to-prepare lunch or supper dish, there is a recipe here to suit.

Tortillas make a great light alternative to bread, lending themselves to almost any hot or cold filling. They can be rolled and easily transported for picnics and packed lunches and are a great choice for informal eating, where everyone can fill their own. Tortillas are the obvious choice for a wrap but this selection also includes stylish vegetable wraps, using peppers, aubergines and courgettes; French-style savoury crêpes; Asian rice-paper and wonton wraps; and Japanese nori for sushi wraps.

Although you can buy ready-prepared wraps, making your own allows you to use the freshest of ingredients, indulge your favourite tastes and control your calorie and fat intake. Tortilla wraps and chapattis are readily available in the supermarkets but I have included recipes for different sizes if you wish to make your own. Do experiment with herbs and spices to add flavour – there is nothing better than freshly made wraps filled while still warm from the pan! Just make sure you match the size of the wrap in the recipe to the size you make or purchase, or adjust the filling ingredients accordingly.

Asian wraps for spring rolls, wonton wraps and mandarin pancakes are readily available from specialist stores and can be frozen. Crêpes are quick and easy to prepare and can be made in advance.

light bites

Buckwheat, with its distinctive earthy flavour, is the essential ingredient for blinis – the celebrated Russian pancakes traditionally served with caviar. These wraps are a variation on blinis, filled with smoked salmon, scrambled egg and asparagus. You could also add a little caviar or lumpfish roe, if wished.

buckwheat pancake wraps

50 g asparagus tips

4 eggs

4 tablespoons milk

15 g butter

75 g smoked salmon, cut into strips

2 tablespoons fresh dill, chopped

8 x 15 cm Buckwheat Pancakes, warmed (see page 63)

salt and freshly ground black pepper

fresh dill sprigs, to garnish

makes 8 serves 4

Blanch the asparagus in lightly salted water for 2 minutes. Drain, then refresh under cold water and pat dry. Cut the asparagus into 2.5 cm lengths.

Beat the eggs together with the milk and season with a little salt and plenty of black pepper. Melt the butter in a non-stick pan, add the egg mixture and cook over a gentle heat, stirring until just starting to set. Stir in the asparagus and cook until the eggs are just scrambled. Fold in the smoked salmon and dill.

Fold the pancakes into quarters and fill with the scrambled egg mix. Put two pancakes on each serving plate, garnish with sprigs of dill and serve immediately.

Halloumi is a Greek cheese which is fairly bland so lends itself to marinating with Mediterranean herbs before wrapping with pieces of char-grilled pepper. It is important to serve these hot while the cheese is soft as it becomes rubbery once cold.

halloumi and pepper wraps with salsa verde

2 tablespoons olive oil

grated zest and freshly squeezed juice of 1 lemon

1 teaspoon balsamic vinegar

2 teaspoons fresh thyme, chopped

225 g halloumi cheese, cut into 12 slices

1 large yellow pepper, halved lengthways

2 large red peppers, halved lengthways

freshly ground black pepper

salsa verde

3 tablespoons olive oil

1 garlic clove, finely chopped

5 cm cucumber, deseeded and finely chopped

grated zest and freshly squeezed juice of 1 lime

2 tablespoons fresh flat leaf parsley, chopped

2 tablespoons fresh basil, chopped

1 teaspoon capers, rinsed and chopped

1 green chilli, finely chopped (optional)

makes 12 serves 4

Preheat the grill to medium.

Mix the olive oil, lemon zest and juice, balsamic vinegar, thyme and black pepper together in a shallow dish. Add the slices of halloumi and set aside to marinate while preparing the peppers.

Put the peppers on the grill rack, skin-side up, and cook until they begin to soften and char. Do not over-cook as they will be cooked again after wrapping. Place in a large bowl, cover and leave for 15 minutes. Meanwhile, mix the salsa verde ingredients together, adding the chilli if wished, and set aside to infuse.

Peel the skins off the peppers and remove the stalks and cores. Cut in half lengthways. Put a slice of halloumi in the centre of each pepper strip, allowing the cheese to protrude slightly over the edges of the pepper. Wrap the pepper over the cheese and secure with a cocktail stick. Put on a shallow baking sheet and brush with the remaining marinade.

Cook under a preheated medium-high grill for 4–5 minutes on each side, or until the cheese softens and starts to brown and the peppers start to char. Serve three pepper wraps per person, drizzled with a little salsa verde.

Chapattis are unleavened breads typically served as an accompaniment to spicy dishes in northern India, so they make the perfect wraps for this spicy Indian chicken topped with yoghurt and cucumber relish.

Indian chicken wraps with minted cucumber relish

250 g skinless chicken breast fillets

2 tablespoons tandoori or tikka masala curry paste

3 tablespoons natural yoghurt

2 teaspoons sunflower oil

4 x 17 cm Chapattis (see page 62)

20 g baby spinach leaves

minted cucumber relish

150 g natural yoghurt

¼ cucumber, deseeded and diced

3 spring onions, chopped

2 tablespoons fresh mint, chopped

½ teaspoon ground cumin

freshly ground black pepper

makes 8 serves 4

Preheat the oven to 200°C (400°F) Gas 6.

Cut the chicken fillets into strips. In a shallow dish, mix the curry paste, yoghurt and oil together. Add the chicken and toss to coat. Cover and leave to marinate for 30 minutes, or up to 4 hours, if time allows.

To make the relish, put the yoghurt into a bowl with the cucumber, spring onions, mint and cumin. Mix together and season with black pepper. Chill.

Transfer the chicken pieces to a non-stick baking tray and bake for 15 minutes, or until the chicken juices run clear. Meanwhile, wrap the chapattis in foil and place in the oven to warm for the last 5 minutes, while the chicken is cooking.

Cut the chapattis in half. Top each half with a few strips of chicken and some spinach leaves, roll up and secure with a cocktail stick. Serve 2 per person, along with a spoonful of the minted cucumber relish.

Spring rolls are best served immediately after cooking, but to keep last-minute preparation minimal make the filling up to 24 hours ahead. Fill the spring roll wrappers about an hour before cooking, but keep them covered so they remain moist until cooked.

mini spring rolls with chilli dipping sauce

2 tablespoons sunflower oil
50 g carrots, cut into matchsticks
50 g mangetouts, cut into matchsticks
50 g shiitake mushrooms, chopped
2.5 cm fresh ginger, peeled and grated
1 small red chilli, deseeded and chopped
50 g bean sprouts
2 spring onions, thinly sliced
1 tablespoon light soy sauce
2 teaspoons plain flour
8 x 20 cm square spring-roll wrappers
oil for deep-frying
a deep-fat fryer

chilli dipping sauce

5 tablespoons sweet chilli sauce
1 tablespoon light soy sauce

makes 16 serves 4

Heat the sunflower oil in a wok or frying pan and stir-fry the carrots, mangetouts, mushrooms and ginger for 1 minute. Add the chilli, bean sprouts and spring onions and stir-fry for 1–2 minutes, or until the vegetables are tender-crisp. Remove from the heat, stir in the soy sauce and set aside to cool.

Next, make the chilli dipping sauce. Mix together the sweet chilli sauce and soy sauce in a small bowl and transfer to a serving dish.

In a small bowl, mix the plain flour with 1 tablespoon water to make a paste. Cut the spring-roll wrappers in half diagonally and place under a damp cloth to keep moist. Remove one at a time to fill.

Divide the filling into four and put a quarter of one batch on the long cut side of a wrapper, placing it along the centre, slightly in from the edge. Fold over the side flaps. Brush a little flour paste on the pointed end of the wrapper and roll up towards the point, pressing the end to seal. Repeat with the remaining wrappers. Keep covered until ready to cook.

Fill a deep-fryer with oil to the manufacturer's recommended level. Heat the oil to 180°C (350°F) and deep-fry the rolls in batches for 2–3 minutes, until crisp and golden. Drain on kitchen paper. Serve hot with the chilli dipping sauce.

3 lemongrass stalks

200 g minced lamb

2 shallots, finely chopped

2 teaspoons fresh parsley, chopped

2 teaspoons fresh coriander, chopped

½ teaspoon ground allspice

1 small red chilli, deseeded and finely chopped

flour, for dusting

2 tablespoons sunflower oil

½ small red pepper, deseeded and cut into thin strips

12 white mini pitta, warmed

12 crisp baby lettuce leaves

12 small sprigs fresh coriander

minted crème fraîche

125 ml half-fat crème fraîche

2 tablespoons fresh mint, chopped

salt and freshly ground black pepper

makes 12 serves 4

These fragrant mini-kebabs are popular in Morocco and Tunisia. The lemongrass skewers add a fragrance and opulence to the koftas, but you can use pre-soaked wooden cocktail sticks if preferred.

lamb kofta wraps with minted crème fraîche

Slice the lemongrass in half widthways, then lengthways to make 12 sticks. In a bowl, mix the minced lamb, shallots, parsley, coriander, allspice and chilli together. Divide into twelve and with lightly floured hands shape into 5 cm long finger shapes. Thread the koftas onto the lemongrass skewers.

In a small bowl mix the crème fraîche and mint together and season with salt and freshly ground black pepper.

Heat the oil in a frying pan and fry the koftas for 4–5 minutes, turning to brown on all sides. At the same time add the pepper strips and cook for 3–4 minutes, to soften and brown slightly.

Open each pitta bread lengthways, place a lettuce leaf in each and add a kofta, a few strips of red pepper and a sprig of coriander. Serve the wraps with the minted crème fraîche.

3 tablespoons mayonnaise

few drops Tabasco sauce

1 teaspoon sun-dried tomato paste

150–180 g lobster meat or wild
crayfish tails, freshly cooked

4 x 19 cm Wheat-flour Tortilla Wraps
(see page 60)

25 g baby salad leaves with herbs

lemon wedges, to serve

guacamole

1 ripe avocado

1 tablespoon freshly squeezed
lime juice

1 tomato, deseeded and finely chopped

1 garlic clove, crushed

1 spring onion, finely chopped

1 tablespoon fresh coriander, chopped

½ teaspoon chilli powder or ½ chilli,
deseeded and chopped

salt and freshly ground black pepper

makes 8 serves 4

For a special treat I like to make these wraps with fresh lobster, but they are equally delicious when made with wild crayfish tails. If you wish to use fresh lobsters two lobsters weighing 450–500 g should yield sufficient meat for this recipe.

shellfish cocktail wraps
with guacamole

To make the guacamole, cut the avocado in half, remove the stone and peel. Mash the flesh in a bowl with the lime juice, then stir in the tomato, garlic, spring onion, coriander and chilli. Season with salt and freshly ground black pepper.

Mix the mayonnaise, Tabasco and sun-dried tomato paste together in a bowl. If using lobster, chop the meat into bite-sized pieces. Add the lobster or crayfish tails to the bowl and mix together.

Lay the tortilla wraps out on a clean work surface and top each one with guacamole, baby salad leaves and shellfish cocktail. Roll each wrap tightly and cut in half. Serve with lemon wedges.

Griddled courgette slices make an ideal wrap for a stylish appetizer which is packed full of flavour. You can also try Roquefort or dolcelatte cheese as alternatives to the Gorgonzola.

courgette rolls

2 courgettes

2 tablespoons olive oil

1 teaspoon freshly squeezed lemon juice

75 g creamy Gorgonzola cheese

75 g ricotta cheese

30 g walnuts, finely chopped

12 mint leaves

small handful of fresh chives, cut into 5 cm lengths

chilli oil, for sprinkling

freshly ground black pepper

a ridged stove-top grill pan

makes 12 serves 4

Trim the ends off the courgettes and cut a thin slice, lengthways, off each side and discard. Then cut each courgette into six slices lengthways, about 5 mm thick. Mix the olive oil and lemon juice together. Brush over the courgette slices and sprinkle with freshly ground black pepper.

Heat a ridged stove-top grill pan for about 4 minutes, or until hot. Put half the courgette slices in the pan and cook until the underneath has developed brown lines from the ridges in the pan. Turn over and repeat on the other side, but do not overcook or they may split when rolled. Transfer to a plate to cool and cook the remaining courgette slices.

Mix the Gorgonzola and ricotta cheeses together and spread over the courgette slices. Sprinkle each with a few chopped walnuts and place a mint leaf and a few chives at one end, so they overlap the edge. Starting from this end gently roll up.

Arrange on serving plates with the mint and chives uppermost. Serve the rolls sprinkled with a little chilli oil and freshly ground black pepper.

These wraps make the perfect prepare-ahead appetizer, especially since the tabbouleh filling will taste even better than when freshly made. Make the filling up to 24 hours in advance, cover and leave in a cool place for the flavours to infuse. At the last minute just fill the tortilla wraps and serve.

smoked ham and tabbouleh cones

50 g bulgar wheat

2 tablespoons fresh mint, chopped

3 tablespoons fresh parsley, chopped

2 spring onions, finely chopped

5 cm cucumber, halved, deseeded and diced

2 tomatoes, diced

1 garlic clove, crushed

3 tablespoons olive oil

1 tablespoon freshly squeezed lemon juice

4 x 24 cm Garlic and Coriander Wheat-flour Tortilla Wraps (see page 60)

4 large thin slices smoked ham, about 200 g

salt and freshly ground black pepper

makes 8 serves 4

Put the bulgar wheat in a bowl, cover with hot water and leave to soak for 30 minutes. Drain well and tip back into the bowl.

Add the mint, parsley, spring onions, cucumber, tomatoes, garlic, olive oil and lemon juice and toss together. Season with a little salt and freshly ground black pepper. Cover and leave for the flavours to infuse.

Cut the tortilla wraps and slices of ham in half and place a piece of ham on top of each tortilla. Roll up one at a time into cone shapes and fill with some tabbouleh. Secure with a cocktail stick or place seam-side down. Arrange in a serving dish or serve 2 per person in individual bowls.

Flautas are usually made with corn tortillas, but are equally enjoyable made using flour tortillas if you find these easier to buy or make. Whichever you choose, fill and cook in the same way; both are delicious and make the perfect appetizer to serve with drinks.

corn flautas
with tomato salsa

200 g cooked chicken breast fillets

80 g feta cheese, crumbled

2 tablespoons fresh coriander, chopped

4 spring onions, chopped

1 small red chilli, deseeded and finely chopped

8 x 15 cm Corn Tortillas (see page 61)

sunflower oil, for frying

soured cream, to serve

tomato salsa

200 g cherry tomatoes, roughly chopped

½ onion, finely chopped

1 tablespoon fresh coriander, chopped

grated zest and freshly squeezed juice of ½ lime

1 tablespoon olive oil

1 mild red chilli e.g. jalapeño, chopped (optional)

makes 16 serves 4–6

To make the salsa, put the cherry tomatoes, onion and coriander in a bowl. Add the grated lime zest and juice, olive oil and chilli, if using, and gently mix together. Cover and set aside to allow the flavours to mingle.

Cut the chicken into thin strips. In a bowl, mix together the chicken, feta cheese, coriander, spring onions and chilli. Wrap the tortillas in foil and warm in the oven, to soften, or wrap in microwave clingfilm and heat for about 30–45 seconds in a microwave oven.

Place a spoonful of chicken filling on one edge of each tortilla and roll up into flutes, tucking the ends in. Secure with a cocktail stick. Cover with clingfilm until ready to cook, to prevent them drying out.

Heat a heavy-based non-stick frying pan filled with oil to a depth of about 2.5 cm, until the oil is hot. Add half the flautas and fry for about 3 minutes, until crisp and golden, turning frequently. Drain on kitchen paper and keep hot while cooking the remaining flautas.

Remove the cocktail sticks, cut each flauta in half diagonally and serve with the tomato salsa and soured cream.

125 g crab meat

50 g cooked and shelled prawns, chopped

4 canned water chestnuts, finely chopped

2 spring onions, finely chopped

2.5 cm fresh ginger, peeled and grated

1 small chilli, deseeded and finely chopped

1 tablespoon fresh coriander, chopped

1 tablespoon light soy sauce

20 x 8–9 cm round wonton wrappers

toasted sesame seeds, to sprinkle

a steamer

soy and ginger dipping sauce

3 tablespoons light soy sauce

3 tablespoons Chinese rice wine or dry sherry

1 cm fresh ginger, peeled and sliced

makes 20 serves 4–6

These bite-sized morsels are typical of Chinese dim sum – they look elegant, smell tantalizing and taste good! Use fresh crab meat for the very best flavour. If you do need to use frozen crab meat, make sure it is well drained before using.

crab wonton wraps with dipping sauce

In a bowl mix together the crab meat, prawns, water chestnuts, spring onions, ginger, chilli, coriander and soy sauce.

Brush the edges of a wonton wrapper with water. Place a heaped teaspoon of filling in the centre. Draw up the edges and press together. Repeat to make 20 wonton wraps. Cover until ready to cook.

In a small bowl, combine the dipping sauce ingredients.

Put a layer of silicone paper in the base of a steamer and arrange the wonton wraps in the steamer, making sure they do not touch each other. Place over a pan of boiling water, cover and steam for 5 minutes. Cook in batches if necessary.

Sprinkle with toasted sesame seeds and serve with the soy and ginger dipping sauce.

simple meals

This recipe serves 4 but easily lends itself to making for just 1 or 2 for a midday meal, just reduce the quantities to suit. Any remaining avocado will keep for up to 24 hours, if left attached to the skin and stone. Brush a little lemon juice over the cut surface to help prevent discoloration.

6 rashers back bacon

2 teaspoons wholegrain mustard

4 tablespoons extra virgin olive oil

1 tablespoon freshly squeezed lemon juice

60 g baby spinach leaves

1 ripe avocado, stoned, peeled and sliced

4 x 24 cm Mediterranean Herb Wheat-flour Tortilla Wraps (see page 60)

150 g ripe brie, sliced

salt and freshly ground black pepper

cranberry-and-onion chutney or cranberry sauce, to serve

makes 4 serves 4

avocado, brie and bacon wraps

Preheat the grill to medium.

Put the bacon rashers on the wire rack of the grill pan and grill for 3–4 minutes per side or until cooked and the fat is golden and crisp. Drain on kitchen paper and cut into pieces with scissors.

Put the mustard, olive oil and lemon juice in a small bowl. Add salt and pepper to season and whisk to make a dressing.

Put the spinach in a bowl, add the bacon and avocado, then pour over the dressing and toss lightly to coat. Divide the salad between the wraps and top with brie slices. Fold one end of each tortilla to enclose the filling, then roll up and serve immediately with chutney or cranberry sauce.

Corn tortillas, pinto beans and chillies are synonymous with Mexican cooking. This recipe combines chicken with a fiery tomato sauce as a filling for the soft tortillas, which are topped with soured cream and Cheddar cheese before baking. It makes a perfect lunch or supper dish served with a crisp leaf salad.

3 tablespoons sunflower oil

450 g skinless chicken breast fillets, cut into strips

1 large onion, chopped

1 red chilli, deseeded and finely chopped

1 garlic clove, crushed

2 tablespoons tomato purée

400 g can chopped tomatoes

410 g can pinto beans, rinsed and drained

1 tablespoon chopped fresh coriander

8 x 19 cm Corn Tortillas, warmed (see page 61)

150 ml soured cream

75 g mature Cheddar cheese, grated

salt and freshly ground black pepper

shredded spring onions, to sprinkle

serves 4–6

chilli chicken enchiladas

Preheat the oven to 190°C (375°F) Gas 5.

Heat 2 tablespoons of the oil in a large non-stick frying pan, add the chicken and stir-fry for 4–5 minutes, or until golden. Remove with a slotted spoon, put into a bowl and set aside.

Add the remaining oil to the pan, then the onion and fry for 5 minutes. Add the chilli and garlic and fry for 1–2 minutes more, or until the onions are soft and golden. Stir in the tomato purée, canned tomatoes and 100 ml cold water. Cook for 2–3 minutes and season with salt and freshly ground black pepper.

Add just under half the sauce to the chicken with the beans and coriander and mix together. Spoon 2 heaped tablespoons of the chicken mixture onto the middle of each warmed tortilla and roll up to enclose the filling. Place seam-side down in a greased baking dish and top with the remaining tomato sauce.

Spoon the soured cream along the centre of the tortillas and sprinkle with the grated cheese. Bake in the preheated oven for 15–20 minutes or until golden and bubbling. Sprinkle over the spring onions and serve.

This mustard and honey-glazed steak makes a succulent and tasty filling for the salsa-flavoured wraps. To make them less messy to eat, serve them 'fajita style', made by enclosing the filling at one end, to form a pocket. Serve one per person for lunch or allow two for a more substantial supper dish along with an extra bowl of salad.

mustard and honey-glazed steak fajitas

2 tablespoons extra virgin olive oil

2 tablespoons clear honey

1 tablespoon balsamic vinegar

2 tablespoons Dijon mustard

2 x 175 g sirloin or rump steaks

3 tablespoons mayonnaise

4 x 24 cm Salsa Wheat-flour Tortilla Wraps (see page 60)

50 g frisée lettuce

4 spring onions, thinly sliced

8 small vine tomatoes, quartered

freshly ground black pepper

a ridged stove-top grill pan (optional)

makes 4 serves 2–4

Preheat the oven to 180°C (350°F) Gas 4. In a shallow dish, mix together the olive oil, honey, balsamic vinegar and 1 tablespoon of the mustard with a generous sprinkling of freshly ground black pepper. Trim the steaks of any fat or sinew, then add to the marinade, turning them over to coat both sides. Cover and leave in a cool place to marinate for 30 minutes, or longer if time allows. Mix the remaining mustard and the mayonnaise together.

Wrap the tortillas in foil and warm them in the oven for 10 minutes. (You can also warm the tortilla wraps in a microwave oven for about 45–60 seconds. If you do, cook the steaks first.)

Heat a heavy-based frying pan or ridged stove-top grill pan until hot, then cook the steaks for 1½–2 minutes each side, or longer if you prefer your steak well done. Slice the steaks.

Divide the lettuce, spring onions and tomatoes between the four tortilla wraps and top with the steak slices. Fold in the sides of the wrap to overlap and then tuck one end underneath to enclose the bottom of the filling. Serve topped with a spoonful of mustard mayonnaise or serve it separately.

These Moroccan-inspired wraps are perfect for an informal lunch. Serve the kebabs, a dish of couscous and a pile of chapatti wraps and invite your guests to help themselves.

3 tablespoons olive oil

1 teaspoon freshly squeezed lemon juice

1 teaspoon ground coriander

½ teaspoon ground turmeric

1 teaspoon harissa paste

550 g lamb leg steaks

2 small red onions, each cut into 8 wedges

125 g couscous

200 ml boiling vegetable stock

8 x 17 cm Chapattis (see page 62)

4 spring onions, shredded

8 ready-to-eat dried apricots, chopped

2 miniature preserved lemons, thinly sliced

25 g toasted flaked almonds

1 tablespoon chopped fresh coriander

8 wooden skewers, soaked in water

harissa dressing

150 ml natural yoghurt

2 teaspoons harissa paste

1 tablespoon chopped fresh coriander

salt and freshly ground black pepper

makes 8 serves 4

lamb and couscous salad wraps with harissa dressing

In a shallow dish mix 2 tablespoons of the olive oil, the lemon juice, ground coriander, turmeric and harissa paste together. Cut the lamb into chunks, add to the dish, toss to coat, cover and leave to marinate in a cool place for 30 minutes or longer, if time allows. Next make the harissa dressing: in a small bowl, mix together the yoghurt, harissa paste and coriander and season with salt and freshly ground black pepper.

Preheat the grill to medium. Thread the chunks of lamb onto the skewers with the onion wedges. Place on a grill rack and brush with the remaining marinade. Put the couscous in a saucepan, pour over the hot stock, cover and let stand for 10 minutes, stirring occasionally.

Put the kebabs under the preheated grill and cook for 8–10 minutes, until browned on the outside but pink in the centre.

Warm the chapattis in a microwave oven for 1–1½ minutes, or in a warm oven, wrapped in foil. Heat the couscous for 1–2 minutes to warm through. Stir in the remaining olive oil, the spring onions, apricots, lemons, almonds and coriander.

Either serve the warm chapattis with the kebabs, couscous and dressing separately, or assemble first by topping each chapatti with a little couscous, then the meat and onions from a kebab. Drizzle the dressing over, before rolling up and securing with a cocktail stick if wished.

Quails' eggs are the perfect size for these summery salad wraps but you can always substitute two hard-boiled hens' eggs cut into wedges if preferred.

salade Niçoise crêpe wraps

2 x 110 g tuna steaks

1 tablespoon olive oil

8 quails' eggs

12 baby new potatoes, halved

75 g French beans, halved

6 baby plum tomatoes on the vine, halved

8 pitted black olives, halved

4 anchovy fillets, cut into thin strips

½ small red onion, thinly sliced

5 tablespoons basil oil

1 tablespoon freshly squeezed lemon juice

8 Crêpes (see page 63)

2 tablespoons freshly grated Parmesan cheese

salt and freshly ground black pepper

a ridged stove-top grill pan

makes 8 serves 4

Heat a ridged stove-top grill pan until hot. Brush the tuna with olive oil and season with freshly ground black pepper. Cook the tuna for 2–3 minutes per side and then set aside to cool. Cook the eggs in boiling water for 3 minutes, or until hard-boiled. Plunge into cold water, shell and cut in half.

Cook the potatoes in boiling, lightly salted water for 6 minutes, add the beans and cook for 4 minutes, or until both are tender. Drain and refresh in cold water and drain well.

In a bowl, toss together the potatoes, beans, tomatoes, olives, anchovies and onion. Whisk 3 tablespoons of the basil oil with the lemon juice and pour over the salad ingredients. Cut the tuna into thick strips and add these and the eggs to the salad. Gently toss together.

Fold the crêpes into four and fill with the salade Niçoise mixture. Arrange on 4 serving plates, drizzle over the remaining basil oil, sprinkle with the Parmesan cheese and serve.

Fennel, peppers and sage, with their distinctive Mediterranean flavours, topped with melted strings of mozzarella provide the succulent filling for these courgette crêpe rolls. You could also use Taleggio or Fontina cheese, both of which will ooze deliciously out of the crêpes as you cut into them.

Mediterranean vegetable crêpe rolls

1 red pepper, deseeded and cut into thick strips

1 orange pepper, deseeded and cut into thick strips

2 onions, cut into wedges

1 fennel bulb, cut into wedges

3 tablespoons olive or sunflower oil

1 garlic clove, crushed

8 Courgette Crêpes (see page 63)

2 teaspoons chopped fresh sage

75 g mozzarella cheese, sliced

50 g Cheddar or Parmesan cheese, grated

25 g fresh breadcrumbs

salt and freshly ground black pepper

makes 8 serves 4

Preheat the oven to 190°C (375°F) Gas 5.

Toss the peppers, onions and fennel together with the oil and garlic and set aside. Make the courgette crêpes and keep them warm by wrapping them in a clean tea towel while you make the filling.

Heat a large griddle pan until hot and cook the vegetables over a medium heat for about 8–10 minutes, or until they are just tender and beginning to char slightly. Stir in the sage and season with salt and freshly ground black pepper.

Divide the vegetables between the crêpes, top with the mozzarella and roll up to enclose the filling. Arrange in a shallow ovenproof dish and sprinkle over the Cheddar or Parmesan cheese and breadcrumbs.

Bake for 15–20 minutes, or until the cheese has melted. If preferred, finish under a preheated grill for about 5 minutes.

These pancake rolls convey the essence of the renowned Peking duck, but with the preparation cut to the minimum. To simplify serving, and make for a very sociable meal, just serve dishes of duck strips, cucumber, spring onions and sauce with the warm pancakes and each person can make their own.

mandarin pancake rolls with duck

3 x 200 g duck breasts

1 tablespoon clear honey

1 teaspoon soy sauce

12–16 mandarin pancakes for crispy duck

120 ml hoisin or plum sauce

10 spring onions, cut in half widthways, then sliced lengthways

½ cucumber, cut into batons about 10 cm long

salt

100 ml sweet chilli sauce, to serve (optional)

a bamboo steamer (optional)

makes 12–16 serves 4

Preheat the oven to 200°C (400°F) Gas 6.

Rub the skin-side of the duck breasts with salt. Leave uncovered in the fridge for at least 2 but up to 8 hours, if time allows, to draw out the moisture. Wipe dry and prick all over with a fork.

Heat a frying pan until hot and cook the duck breasts skin-side down for 5 minutes, drawing off the fat as it is released. Transfer to a rack in a roasting tin, placing the skin side uppermost, and roast for 10 minutes. Meanwhile mix the honey and soy sauce together.

Brush the honey mixture over the duck and cook for 5–10 minutes more, depending how well cooked you like duck. Leave to rest for 5 minutes, then cut into strips. Warm the mandarin pancakes in a bamboo steamer over simmering water or stack on a plate, cover with foil and place the plate over a pan of simmering water.

To serve, spread a little hoisin sauce on each pancake, fill with a few duck strips, spring onion strips and cucumber batons and roll up. Serve immediately with sweet chilli sauce, if wished.

Serve these translucent oriental-style wraps with a vegetable stir-fry. Just stir-fry a combination of baby pak choi, cut in half lengthways, sugar snap peas and shiitake mushrooms with a little crushed garlic while you are cooking the wraps.

salmon in rice-paper wraps

4 x 100 g salmon fillets

grated zest and freshly squeezed juice of 1 lime

4 cm fresh ginger, peeled and grated

2 tablespoons fresh coriander, chopped

4 spring onions, chopped

1 garlic clove, crushed

8 x 20 cm Vietnamese rice-paper pancakes

4 tablespoons sunflower oil

4 tablespoons Thai fish sauce or oyster sauce

1 tablespoon toasted sesame seeds

makes 8 serves 4

Cut each piece of salmon in half. Mix the lime juice and zest, ginger, coriander, spring onions and garlic together in a bowl. Spread over the tops of the salmon pieces.

Fill a shallow dish large enough to hold the rice-paper pancakes with warm water. Soak them for 15–20 seconds or until just soft and pliable. Place on a damp tea towel and blot to remove excess water. Place a piece of fish on each round. Fold in the sides of the pancakes and roll to enclose and wrap the fish.

Heat the oil in a frying pan over a medium heat. Add the fish parcels and fry for 2–3 minutes per side, or until the rice paper is golden and the fish is just tender. Drain on kitchen paper.

Arrange two rice-paper wraps on each serving plate, drizzle over a little Thai fish sauce and sprinkle with sesame seeds. Serve with stir-fried vegetables, if wished.

food on the go

Outdoor feasts are always occasions to enjoy. The combination of wafer-thin slices of Parma ham, pecorino cheese, juicy ripe peaches and fresh rocket leaves makes a perfect blend of flavours for a summer eating experience worth savouring.

2 tablespoons pesto sauce

125 g curd cheese

4 x 24 cm Wheat-flour Tortilla Wraps
(see page 60)

125 g Parma ham, very thinly sliced

2 ripe peaches, peeled, stoned
and sliced

25 g rocket leaves

25 g pecorino cheese shavings

few fresh basil leaves, to sprinkle

balsamic vinegar and olive oil,
to drizzle

freshly ground black pepper

makes 8 serves 4

Parma ham, peach and pecorino cornets

In a small bowl, mix the pesto sauce and curd cheese together. Spread over the tortilla wraps and then cut each wrap in half.

Tear the Parma ham into smaller pieces. Divide the peach slices, rocket and Parma ham between the wraps and sprinkle with black pepper. Roll each one into a cone shape and secure with a cocktail stick if wished.

Arrange on serving plates and sprinkle over the pecorino cheese shavings and basil leaves. Drizzle with balsamic vinegar and olive oil and serve immediately. If transporting to a picnic, pack in a suitable box and take the olive oil and balsamic vinegar separately to drizzle over just before eating.

Crêpes make wonderful wrappers for savoury fillings and are a great alternative to tortillas. This recipe fuses Western-style crêpes flavoured with spring onions with an oriental crispy vegetable, ginger-marinated pork and hoisin sauce filling.

oriental pork crêpe wraps

2 tablespoons sunflower oil

2 tablespoons soy sauce

4 cm fresh ginger, peeled and grated

2 teaspoons ground coriander

400 g pork fillet, sliced

8 Spring Onion Crêpes (see page 63)

60 g Chinese leaves, shredded

50 g bean sprouts

3 spring onions, cut into fine strips

6 tablespoons hoisin sauce

makes 8 serves 4

In a shallow dish, mix together the oil, soy sauce, ginger and ground coriander. Add the pork slices and toss to coat.

Heat a non-stick frying pan or wok and stir-fry the pork for 3–4 minutes, until cooked. Remove and set aside to cool.

To assemble, fill each crêpe with some Chinese leaves, bean sprouts and spring onions. Top with a few pork slices and some hoisin sauce. Roll up to enclose the filling and tuck one end under, fajita style.

If you are making these for a picnic, spread the hoisin sauce over each crêpe first and then top with the remaining filling ingredients and roll as above.

Aubergine slices make the perfect wrap for easy-to-prepare alfresco eating. Packed with the flavours of the Mediterranean – feta cheese, basil, sun-dried tomatoes and pine nuts – what could be better for an outing on a summer's day?

aubergine rolls

1 large aubergine

2 tablespoons olive oil

½ small red onion

15 g fresh basil leaves

125 g feta cheese, crumbled

4 sun-blushed tomatoes in oil, drained and chopped

50 g pine nuts, toasted

freshly ground black pepper

a ridged stove-top grill pan

makes 8 serves 4

Trim the stalk off the aubergine and cut lengthways into eight thin slices, about 5 mm thick. Heat a ridged stove-top grill pan until it is really hot. Brush both sides of the aubergine slices with oil and cook, in batches, for 1½–2 minutes on each side, until tender and soft enough to roll up. Set aside to cool.

Cut the onion into thin slivers, lengthways. Reserve a few small leaves of basil and shred the remainder. In a bowl gently toss the feta cheese, tomatoes, shredded basil and 40 g pine nuts together and season with freshly ground black pepper.

Pile a spoonful of the feta mix on the end third of each aubergine slice and add a few slivers of onion. Roll up and place seam-side down on a serving plate or pack in a picnic container. Serve sprinkled with the remaining pine nuts and reserved basil leaves.

I like the contrast of the tart peppery note of the watercress with the sweet juicy mango and spice-laced basmati rice in these chapatti wraps. If you prefer, you could replace the watercress with a mixed-leaf salad such as mixed baby leaves or a mustard-leaf salad.

fragrant rice with mango and turkey wraps

generous pinch of saffron

300 ml hot chicken stock

3 tablespoons sunflower oil

175 g turkey breast, cut into strips

2 shallots, chopped

75 g basmati rice

3 cardamom pods, crushed, black seeds retained and the pods discarded

2 cloves

½ stick cinnamon

4 tablespoons mayonnaise

2 teaspoons curry paste

4 x 20 cm Chapattis (see page 62)

15 g cashew nuts, toasted

1 ripe mango, peeled, stoned and cut into small slices

20–25 g watercress

freshly ground black pepper

makes 8 serves 4

Stir the saffron into the hot stock and set aside. Heat 2 tablespoons of the oil in a frying pan, add the turkey strips and shallots and sauté for 3–4 minutes to brown slightly.

Meanwhile, heat the remaining oil in a non-stick saucepan, add the rice and cook, stirring, for 1 minute. Add the cardamom seeds, cloves and cinnamon and cook for 1 minute more.

Pour in the saffron stock and bring to the boil. Add the turkey and shallots, season with black pepper, cover and cook gently for about 12 minutes, or until the rice is tender and all the liquid has been absorbed. Remove the cloves and cinnamon stick, discard and set the rice aside to cool.

Mix the mayonnaise and curry paste together and spread over the chapattis. Stir the cashew nuts into the rice and then put a quarter of the rice mix on each chapatti and top with mango slices and watercress. Roll up firmly to enclose the filling and cut in half to serve. If the wraps are to go, wrap in clingfilm and place in a picnic box.

Tortillas, which originated from Latin America, are perfect for picnics and packed lunches as an alternative to a sandwich. These flat breads can be wrapped around almost any filling; here I have wrapped crisp vegetables inside a tortilla spread with garlicky hummus.

lemon and garlic hummus tortilla rolls

410 g can chickpeas, rinsed and drained

grated zest and freshly squeezed juice of 1 lemon

2 garlic cloves, chopped

30 ml extra virgin olive oil

1 tablespoon tahini paste

4 x 24 cm Wheat-flour Tortilla Wraps (see page 60)

2 carrots, cut into thin sticks

2 celery sticks, chopped

4 sun-dried tomatoes in oil, drained and sliced

½ small onion, thinly sliced

50 g lamb's lettuce

salt and freshly ground black pepper

makes 8 serves 4

To make the hummus, put the drained chickpeas in a food processor with the lemon juice, garlic and olive oil. Blend until semi-smooth before adding the tahini. Season with salt and pepper and blend until smooth. Finally, stir in the grated lemon zest.

Lay the tortilla wraps on a clean work surface and spread a quarter of the hummus over each. Divide the carrots, celery, sun-dried tomatoes, onion and lamb's lettuce between the tortilla wraps, scattering over the centre in a band. Season and tightly roll up each wrap.

Cut each wrap in half and serve or wrap in baking parchment and pack into a picnic box.

These wraps are best made as close to eating as possible, ideally within an hour as the nori will soften once filled. For a hands-on picnic, take separate containers of the individual ingredients, plus the cooked rice and nori sheets, and let everyone make their own wraps, choosing their favourite fillings.

sushi wraps

225 g Japanese short-grain rice

2 tablespoons rice vinegar

1 tablespoon mirin

$\frac{1}{2}$ teaspoon caster sugar

$\frac{1}{2}$ teaspoon salt

$\frac{1}{2}$ small avocado

1 tablespoon freshly squeezed lemon juice

4 sheets nori, each cut into four

2 tablespoons wasabi paste

100 g fresh tuna fillet, cut into 8 fingers

$\frac{1}{2}$ yellow pepper, deseeded and cut into sticks

50 g smoked salmon slices, cut into 8 pieces

8 cooked and shelled tiger prawns

6 cm cucumber, cut into sticks

pickled ginger and shoyu sauce, to serve

makes 16 serves 4

Put the rice in a non-stick saucepan with 330 ml cold water, bring to the boil, cover tightly and cook over a very low heat for 12 minutes. Remove from the heat and leave to stand for 15 minutes. Mix the rice vinegar, mirin, sugar and salt together and fold into the rice. Cover and leave to cool.

Cut the avocado into slices. Put the lemon juice in a shallow dish, add the avocado and toss to coat.

Spread 2 tablespoons of rice over a piece of nori. Add a small amount of wasabi paste and top with a piece each of tuna, pepper and avocado. You may find this easier if you hold the nori on the palm of your hand to fill. Roll up into a cone shape. Dampen the final edge with water or shoyu sauce to stick together. Fill 7 more squares of nori in the same way.

Fill the remaining nori squares with rice topped with a smoked salmon piece, a prawn and a couple of cucumber sticks. Serve the sushi wraps with small dishes of ginger and shoyu sauce.

I have included the recipe for Caesar dressing, which is certainly worth the effort for the very best flavour and really only takes a few minutes to make. If, however, you are short of time for a spur-of-the-moment picnic, make sure you use the best quality ready-prepared Caesar dressing you can find.

75 g Parmesan cheese

4 x 24 cm Wheat-flour Tortilla Wraps (see page 60)

8–12 cos lettuce or romaine heart lettuce leaves, depending on size

300 g cooked skinless chicken fillets, sliced

Caesar dressing

2 garlic cloves, chopped

2 anchovy fillets in oil, drained and chopped

1 egg yolk

1 tablespoon white wine vinegar

1 tablespoon Dijon mustard

50 ml light olive oil

50 ml sunflower oil

freshly ground black pepper

makes 8 serves 4

chicken Caesar salad wraps with Caesar dressing

To prepare the Caesar dressing, mash the garlic and anchovies to a paste in a small bowl. Put in a food processor with the egg yolk, vinegar, mustard and a little black pepper. Blend together briefly, then, with the motor still running, add the oils in a slow trickle through the feed tube, as if you were making mayonnaise.

Use a potato peeler to make Parmesan cheese shavings. Lay the tortilla wraps out on a clean work surface and top each one with 2–3 lettuce leaves, a few chicken breast slices and some Parmesan shavings. Drizzle with Caesar dressing.

Roll each wrap tightly and cut in half diagonally. Wrap in baking parchment and pack into a picnic box or serve as required.

The flavour of the toasted sesame seeds in the crêpes complements the ginger and chilli flavoured prawns, but they are equally delicious wrapped in spring onion-flavoured or wholewheat crêpes.

sesame crêpe wraps and piquant prawns with aioli

32 large uncooked tiger prawns, shelled and de-veined, tails on

1 lemongrass stalk, chopped

4 cm fresh ginger, peeled and chopped

1 red chilli, deseeded

4 tablespoons olive oil

1 tablespoon freshly squeezed lemon juice

8 Sesame Crêpes (see page 63)

2 heads of chicory

small bunch fresh flat leaf parsley

garlic and lemon aioli

1 garlic clove, chopped

½ teaspoon salt

grated zest and freshly squeezed juice of ½ lemon

1 egg yolk

60 ml extra virgin olive oil

60 ml sunflower oil

freshly ground black pepper

makes 8 serves 4

Remove the tails from 24 of the prawns and put all the prawns in a shallow dish. Place the lemongrass, ginger, chilli, olive oil and lemon juice in a food processor and blend to a rough paste. Add to the prawns, toss together, cover and leave in the refrigerator to marinate for 30 minutes, or longer if time allows.

To make the aioli, place the garlic, salt, lemon juice and egg yolk in the cleaned food processor and pulse briefly to combine. With the motor running, slowly trickle in the two oils through the feeder tube until the aioli is thick and emulsified. Season with freshly ground black pepper and stir in the lemon zest.

Heat a frying pan until hot, add the prawns and marinade and stir-fry for 2–3 minutes, until the prawns turn pink, but don't over-cook or they will become tough. Set aside to cool.

To assemble, fill each sesame crêpe with 2–3 chicory leaves and top with the prawns, making sure a prawn with its tail is at the top. Scatter over a few sprigs of parsley and roll tightly to enclose the filling. Fold the bottom end under to secure. Serve with the garlic and lemon aioli.

basic recipes

Wheat-flour tortillas are readily available, but if you make them, you can add your favourite herbs and spices. They are more pliable than corn tortillas, but it is worth warming them slightly (even for a cold fill) to assist in the rolling and folding and prevent cracking.

wheat-flour tortilla wraps

250 g plain white flour

½ teaspoon salt

50 g vegetable fat or lard

150–160 ml lukewarm water

makes 9–10 x 19 cm, 8 x 21 cm or 6 x 24 cm

Variations

Garlic and Coriander
Add 2 crushed garlic cloves and 1 tablespoon finely chopped fresh coriander.

Mediterranean Herb
Add 1 tablespoon each finely chopped fresh oregano and flat leaf parsley.

Salsa
Mix 4 teaspoons tomato purée with half the water, and add enough of the remaining water to mix to a dough. Add 1 teaspoon chilli powder, 1 crushed garlic clove, 2 teaspoons finely chopped fresh flat leaf parsley and 1 tablespoon finely chopped fresh oregano.

Mix the flour and salt together in a large bowl. Rub in the vegetable fat or lard using your fingertips. Stir in enough water to mix to a smooth dough. Knead for 3–4 minutes, then place in a clean bowl, cover and leave to rest for 15 minutes. If adding any flavourings, knead into the dough before leaving to rest.

Divide into individual pieces depending on the size you wish to make. On a lightly floured surface roll out each piece of dough, very thinly, into rounds of your selected size. Keep the dough balls and rolled tortillas covered so they stay moist.

Heat a large heavy-based griddle or frying pan until hot and cook the tortillas, one at a time, for 1½–2 minutes, turning over as soon as the surface starts to bubble. Take care not to over-cook; they should stay soft and flexible, otherwise they will break when rolled. Wrap the cooked tortillas in a clean tea towel to keep them soft and warm, while you cook the rest.

To re-warm tortillas, place on a microwave-proof plate, wrap with microwave clingfilm and microwave for about 10 seconds for one, or 30 seconds for four. To warm in the oven, wrap in aluminium foil and place in a preheated oven at 180°C (350°F) Gas 4 for 10 minutes.

These corn tortillas use masa harina. Distinctive in flavour, it makes a more dense tortilla than the wheat-flour version. For a lighter, easier-to-roll tortilla, replace up to half the masa harina with wheat flour. It is not the same as cornmeal, maize meal or polenta and these cannot be substituted successfully.

corn tortillas

275 g masa harina
½ teaspoon salt
250 ml water
1 tablespoon corn oil

**makes 12 x 15 cm
or 8 x 19 cm**

Place the masa harina, salt, water and oil in a bowl and mix together to a dough. Turn onto a lightly floured surface and knead well for 3–4 minutes, until firm and smooth. Put in a clean bowl, cover and leave to rest for 30 minutes.

Divide the dough into 12 or 8, depending on the size of tortilla you wish to make. Keep covered. Put a ball of dough between two sheets of clingfilm. Flatten gently with the palm of your hand, then roll out into a 15 cm or 19 cm diameter round tortilla, turning a quarter turn with each roll. You can use a tortilla press or chapatti press instead of a rolling pin.

Heat an un-greased griddle or heavy-based frying pan over a moderate heat. Peel off the top layer of clingfilm. Turn the tortilla onto your hand, remove the remaining film and transfer to the pan. Cook for about 45 seconds, or until the underside is blistered and golden speckles are just beginning to appear. Using a spatula, turn over and cook for another 30 seconds.

If using immediately, wrap the cooked tortillas in a clean tea towel or wrap in foil and place in a preheated oven at 150°C (300°F) Gas 2 to keep warm while cooking the remainder.

To reheat, either place on a microwave-proof plate, cover with microwave clingfilm and cook on full power for 40–50 seconds or sprinkle with a little cold water, wrap in foil and place in a preheated oven at 180°C (350°F) Gas 4 for 10 minutes.

These Indian flat breads are traditionally made with a very fine wholemeal flour called atta, sometimes simply labelled chapatti flour. Blended atta flours contain both wholemeal and white flour and give a slightly lighter chapatti. The blended flours are perfect for wraps, as they make the wraps easier to roll.

chapattis

225 g atta or chapatti flour

½ teaspoon salt

140–150 ml water

1 teaspoon vegetable oil

**makes 8 x 17 cm
or 5 x 20 cm**

Put the flour and salt into a bowl. Add the water slowly, adding just enough to mix to a soft dough. Knead in the oil.

Turn onto a lightly floured surface and knead for 5–6 minutes, until smooth. Place in a lightly oiled bowl, cover with a damp tea towel and leave to rest for 30 minutes. On a lightly floured surface, divide the dough into 8, or 5 if making large chapattis, and shape into balls.

Flatten the dough using the palm of your hand, then roll out into a 17 cm or 20 cm round. Stack on top of each other with sheets of clingfilm in between to keep the chapattis moist.

Heat a cast-iron griddle or heavy-based frying pan over a medium heat until hot. Brush any excess flour from the chapattis and place on the griddle or in the pan. Cook for 45 seconds, or until the top side begins to bubble and white specks appear on the underside. Turn over and cook for a further 30–45 seconds. Remove, place on a plate and cover with a clean tea towel to keep moist.

They are best served fresh. To reheat, wrap in foil and place in a preheated oven at 180°C (350°F) Gas 4 for 10 minutes, or sprinkle with a few drops of water, wrap in microwave clingfilm and reheat for a few seconds in the microwave. Allow around 10–15 seconds for one and 40–50 seconds for the whole quantity.

Make a batch of crêpes up to 24 hours in advance so they can be filled and served in minutes. Most recipes in this book use cold crêpes, but if you need to reheat them, wrap the stack of crêpes in foil and place in a preheated oven at 180°C (350°F) Gas 4 for 10 minutes to warm through.

crêpes

115 g plain white flour

pinch of salt

1 egg

about 300 ml milk

sunflower oil for frying

makes 8

Variations

Sesame Crêpes
Add 1 tablespoon lightly toasted sesame seeds to the finished batter.

Buckwheat Pancakes
Use 40 g buckwheat flour and 25 g plain white flour in place of 115 g plain white flour. Reduce the milk to 180 ml.

Spring Onion Crêpes
Stir 2 finely chopped spring onions into the finished batter.

Courgette Crêpes
Stir 125 g grated courgettes and 2 teaspoons chopped fresh thyme into the batter.

Wholewheat Crêpes
Replace half the plain white flour with wholemeal flour.

Sift the flour and salt into a bowl and make a well in the centre. Add the egg and a little of the milk and whisk together, gradually incorporating the flour. Add the remaining milk and mix to a smooth batter. It should have the consistency of thin cream. Pour into a jug and set aside for 30 minutes. If the batter has thickened, add a little extra milk.

Heat a little oil in an 18–20 cm crêpe pan or heavy-based frying pan, or a 15 cm pan if making buckwheat pancakes, until hot. Pour off the excess oil. Add a little batter to the pan, about 3 tablespoons, tilting the pan so the batter is evenly and thinly spread over the bottom of the pan.

Cook over a moderate heat for about 1 minute, or until the underside is golden and the top is set. Flip the crêpe over using a palette knife and cook for a further 30–45 seconds, or until it is golden. Turn onto a sheet of silicone paper and continue until all the batter is used. Stack the pancakes between layers of silicone paper. To keep them warm, cover loosely in foil and place on a baking sheet in the oven at 160°C (325°F) Gas 3.

index